GERMANY
TRAVEL FOR KIDS

www.dinobibi.com

Author: Celia Jenkins
Editor: Kristy Elam
Illustrator: Jacqueline Cacho

CONTENTS

JULI

		1	2	3	4	
5	6	7	8	9	10	
12	13	14	15	16	17	
19	20	21	22	23	24	
26	27	28	29	30	31	

Native Plants & Animals (pg. 22)

Food, Culture, & Traditions (pg. 26)

Famous People (pg. 38)

Major Cities & Attractions (pg. 42)

INTRODUCTION: HELLO FRIENDS!

Guten tag! Good day, it's nice to meet you. Ich bin Hanna Luisa. Do you understand German? I said I am Hanna Luisa, but my friends just call me Hanna. It's quite common for people in Germany to have two first names, but only use the first one. My best friend is Lina Charlotte, but I just call her Lina.

I spend a lot of time with Lina because I'm an only child. Lina's so lucky — she has a brother and a sister. I don't have any! But it's quite common in Germany to be an only child. Lina is of Turkish heritage, and Turkish families often have more children. Three percent of the German population is Turkish, which is a lot of people!

Fun Fact
Only about 75% of people in Germany are actually German.

Popular Names in Germany

So, I just have a family of three, but that's ok. We're very close. Both of my parents have quite traditional German names. Lately, German parents have been choosing names that are more Western and not so German. For example, in my school here are some popular names: Sophia, Emma, Mia, Anna, Ben, Paul, Henry, and Jacob. My name is more traditional and is even spelled the German way — in the UK, they spell it 'Hannah.'

Fun Fact
In 2016, 16% of boys and 17% of girls born were given names listed in the top 10 popular names.

Das Grande
VORNAMEN
Lexicon

As I was saying, my mum's name is Silke, which isn't a very common name at all these days! She has a very typical German job because she works in IT. People used to think that working with computers was a job for boys, and even today many of her colleagues are men. But recently Mama changed to work for a new company, and the boss is a woman. She likes it better there!

My dad is called Sven and he has a much more unusual job. Papa works at the Neanderthal Museum, here in Mettmann where we live. The museum is all about archaeology and is located on the site of the first Neanderthal man discovered in this area. Papa trained as an archaeologist and so he knows all about the exhibits in the museum. He spends a few days a week working in the museum itself. He gives talks and tours and sometimes does other little jobs that need to be done. Other days he is busy in the office doing research, writing academic papers, or even going on archaeological digs to see what can be found. Mama does her job because she needs to earn money, and she's good at it, but Papa chose his job because of pure passion. He loves it, and I think he'd go to work every day of the week, if he could!

Our Family Traditions

I guess we're a pretty traditional family, and we're like our friends and neighbours. Some of my parents' friends are Christian, and some of them aren't. My parents were both brought up in Christian families, but we don't go to church every week because they know I'm an agnostic. Like many people my age (by the way, I'm thirteen years old!) I don't know what I believe yet. But we always go to church at Easter and Christmas because these are special occasions. It's not like I hate religion or anything, I'm just not interested. It's one of my least favourite subjects at school.

In Germany, going to kindergarten is optional. You don't have to start school officially until you're six. My parents decided not to send me to kindergarten until I was five. I think because I'm an only child, they wanted to really enjoy their time with me and teach me a lot of things. At that time, my parents both worked part-time, so they could take turns looking after me. I think I learned a lot more spending time with my parents than in a kindergarten class, because when I started school, I felt a lot smarter than the other kids! But I was shy, because I hadn't spent much time playing with children my own age.

Chemistry

History

Literature

After kindergarten, we have Grundschule, which means ground school. You go to Grundschule from the ages of six to eleven. After that, you have lower secondary school (which I'm in now) and upper secondary. Lower secondary is quite general. I study a lot of different things every week. But in upper secondary, I can make more choices. Many schools in Germany offer special programs that train you specifically for certain jobs. In upper secondary you don't have to waste time studying things you aren't interested in. If you want to, you can specialise in something and do an apprenticeship. But I don't have to worry about that yet!

Before we continue our trip, I would like to know more about you.
Can you please complete this little questionnaire for me?

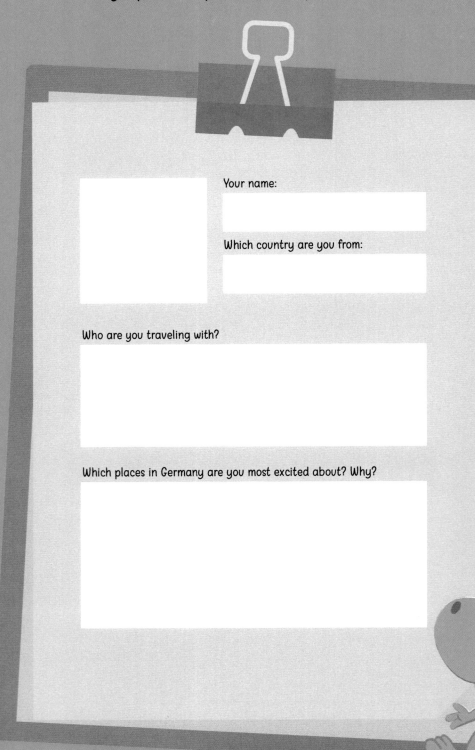

Your name:

Which country are you from:

Who are you traveling with?

Which places in Germany are you most excited about? Why?

GEOGRAPHY OF GERMANY

NORTH SEA

BALTIC SEA

BELGIUM

LUX.

FRANCE

CZECH REPUBLIC

Flensburg

Rostock

Hamburg

Emdem

Oldenberg

Bremen

Berlin

Hannover

Münster

Dortmund

Leipzig

Kassel

Cologne

Dresten

Bonn

Frankfurt

Nürnberg

Regensburg

Heildelberg

Stuttgart

Augsburg

Ulm

Munich

Freiburg

Flying the Flag for Germany

I know you don't speak German, but do you know what Flagge Deutschlands means? If you speak English, it's sometimes easier for you to understand German than it is to understand, for example, French, Spanish, or Italian. That's because English and German are both Germanic languages. They're both West Germanic languages, which makes them even more similar than compared to the North Germanic languages, such as Swedish, Finnish, and Danish. It basically means that those languages have the same roots; although they're different languages, some things are the same.

Anyway... what was I saying? Oh yes! Flagge Deutschlands. Can you guess? It means 'Flag of Germany.' Do you know what it looks like? It's a tricolour flag, like France, but the bands of colour are horizontal, not vertical. The colours of our flag are black, red, and yellow. Those colours have been used since 1867 and were the symbol for Germany during several revolutions and for different republics. There's also a flag that is black, red, and white, but it's not popular because of its connections to World War II.

Do you have flag days in your country? In Germany, on flag days all public buildings must fly the German flag. Mostly, those days are to do with politics or as a memorial to something. One flag day is May 23rd, which is Constitution Day, which we call Grundgesetztag. It's the anniversary of basic German law in 1949. Another flag day is the People's Mourning Day, Volkstrauertag, which is the 2nd Sunday in advent. I like this one because it's a day to remember everybody killed in wartime — not just soldiers, not just Germans, but everyone.

Brandenburg Gate, Berlin, Germany.

Learning About Germany

I've been interested in Germany and my identity as a German since I joined a club called German Studies. It sounds boring, but what it does is link everything together that we study in school. For example, we study history, geography, politics, law, economics... and German Studies brings it all together, and shows how things link up. I joined because my best friend Lina is really interested in geography and wanted to get some extra information. Last year, she got the highest marks in the class for geography and, in the future, she's hoping to get a scholarship for university. Anyway, that's why I go to German Studies club and learn about important things to do with my country.

Recently we've been looking at iconic cities in Germany. I live in Mettmann, which is quite a small town in North Rhine-Westphalia, in the west of Germany. The important cities of Germany are spread all over the country, which makes sense if you think about it! In the north are Bremen, Hanover, and Hamburg, and Berlin, the capital, is sort of north-east. In the east are Dresden and Leipzig. In the south there are big cities like Nuremberg, Stuttgart, and Munich, and then in the west, closer to me, is Frankfurt, Cologne, and Dortmund. Cologne is only a 45-minute drive away, and Dortmund can be reached in an hour, so I've visited these cities many, many times. Mama likes to go shopping in these big cities, particularly at Christmas, so I'm familiar with those places. But I've been to some other big cities in Germany because my school has a lot of trips for students, which I'm lucky to go on.

Germany has quite a big population, about 83 million people! It's a popular place, right? I think there are at least four cities with a population of over a million people, about ten cities with half a million, and dozens of cities that have more than 100,000 people. Because I live in a small place with a population of just 40,000, it's incredible to me! What about you? Is there a big population where you're from?

Fun Fact
German is the official language of Germany, but around 70% of the population can communicate in a foreign language, and around 30% of those can speak in two languages other than German.

Harbor on Lake Constance in Lindau, Germany.

German Lakes

The biggest lake in Germany is Lake Constance, which we call Konstanz. Actually, that's not true. We share Lake Constance with Switzerland and Austria — the lake is in-between us. Konstanz is 63 km (39 mi) long and 14 km (8.7 mi) wide. The average depth is 90 m (300 ft), which seems deep enough to me, but then the deepest parts are 251 m (823 ft) deep. Incredible, right? It must be a whole different world down there! Guess how many shipwrecks there are at the bottom of the lake? There are five! One was an accident after it collided with another ship, and four of them were sunk there after they were taken out of service, which seems like a big waste to me.

Lake Müritz is the largest lake located entirely within German territory. It's a lot shallower, with the maximum depth being just 31 metres (102 ft). However, if you were standing at the bottom of it, I think that it would still seem like the surface was a very long way off! The average depth is just 6 m (20 ft), which is how tall an adult giraffe is... so I guess the giraffe would be underwater. But 6m is just half the height of dinosaur called a Brachiosaurus, so it'd be all right if it wanted to walk through it, haha! Now you can see how interested I am in linking facts to other facts! It's contagious!

13

How much?

The cost of living in Germany is not bad compared to other countries in Western Europe but more expensive than places in Eastern Europe. Many foreigners come to Germany because the standard of living is very good. We have excellent transportation, education, and healthcare systems, and the cost of things isn't super high. As such, living in Berlin can be much cheaper than living in other capital cities like London, Paris, Rome, or Zurich. In 2018, seven German cities featured in the top 30 list of the quality of living survey, three of which were in the top 10: Munich (3rd), Düsseldorf (6th), Frankfurt (7th), Berlin (13th), Hamburg (19th), Nuremberg (23rd), and Stuttgart (28th). It makes a big difference if the cost of living is good, because people are happier and can afford a nicer lifestyle.

Fun Fact
Living in Berlin is estimated to be 34% cheaper compared to living in New York City.

Because I'm an only child, my parents can afford some nice things for us. If I had a brother or sister, we'd have less money, so I guess that's why some parents in Germany choose just to have one child. We do our grocery shopping at places like Lidl and Aldi, which are also popular in other countries, but actually come from Germany. They're called 'discount stores' because things are cheaper than in other shops, but I think the quality is just as good!

14

WEATHER IN GERMANY

Mountain road in Berchtesgaden National Park during winter.

Guten morgen, good morning to you. Do you know much about the geography of Germany? We've been learning about it in German Studies. It's not geography like cities and towns, but geography in relation to weather and stuff like that. Because of climate change, everyone wants to know more about the natural world these days. Myself included! So, I'm really interested in the climate of my country and how it's changed over time.

Germany is a big country, but the weather doesn't vary too much from north to south, or east to west. The western side of Germany has a more temperate climate, whereas the east can be colder. Both sides of Germany have warm summers, though, and cooler winters. And there isn't really a dry season in Germany; we get an average of 789 mm (31 in) of precipitation per year.

I guess it's fair to say that the east is more extreme than the west. They have colder winters and warmer summers, but different places in Germany are fairly similar and have seasonal weather. We don't get much extreme weather, which is a good thing. I don't think it makes your life very comfortable if the weather gets super-duper hot or super-duper cold. The really cold weather in Germany doesn't happen much these days. If you look at a list of extremely cold weather in Germany, here are the years that the top 6 coldest temperatures happened in: 2001, 2005, 1871, 1850, 1929, and 1893. Most those dates are a really long time ago! The most extreme warm weather is much more recent. I think it's because of global warming, and we're seeing extreme heat more regularly now, don't you think? In 2019, Germany saw the highest ever recorded temperature, 41.2 °C (106.2 °F).

Fun Fact

If you look at the dates of the sixteen hottest temperatures ever recorded in Germany, they all happened in recent years. The one longest in the past was in 1992, but most are from the 2000s.

Rainbow over the city of Hamburg, Germany.

Annual Temperatures Around

I like the temperature in Mettmann, where I live. The best weather is in June, July, and August. Average temperatures at that time that fall between 20°C (68°F) and 25°C (77°F), so it's warm but not too hot. But those are also the months when it's most likely to rain, so it's pros and cons! January is the coldest month in Mettmann and April is the driest. I think May is a great time because we get a lot of sunshine at that time of year, even though it isn't really hot yet.

Berlin

Shall I tell you about other places in Germany? I'll tell you about Berlin, our capital. They have the same pleasant temperatures as us in the summer, except that is usually starts around May and continues until September. Lucky for them! June is usually a wet month in Berlin, and October is the driest. Last year, Lina and I went on a school trip to Berlin. We were really unlucky with the weather. We went for five days, and it rained for four of them! I went to Berlin a few years ago with Mama and Papa. We went around Christmas time, actually. It wasn't very rainy but I remember it was bitterly cold. Papa had to buy me a new scarf because I lost mine of the first day of the trip.

The World Clock, located in the public square of Alexanderplatz in Mitte, Berlin.

Average Temperatures

If you want to know when the best time to visit Germany, I couldn't really tell you. I don't think there's a bad time or a good time. All year the weather is pretty good. I guess it depends what kind of weather you like! If you don't like it too hot or too cold, I think the autumn is nice. Lows of 9°C (49°F) are common in September and that drops to 1°C (34°F) in November. For average highs, it's about 19°C (67°F) in September and 8°C (47°F) in November. It usually snows across Germany in the winter so if you don't like snow then perhaps wait until a warmer time of year!

Autumn foliage around Neuschwanstein Castle.

Wind Power

Come rain, sun or snow, something we have a lot of in Germany is wind! Haha, no it's not because we eat too many Brussels sprouts! Windy weather can be a pain if you have long hair, I know, but I don't mind how windy it is here because I know there's a positive side to it. Wind power can be harnessed to use as green energy, replacing bad things like coal and nuclear power. Wind doesn't run out — we always have it! Solar power is a great idea but, you know, it's not always sunny, so it's not so efficient. Whereas the wind in Germany is reliable, so the country has been taking measures to make the most of it.

Germany has both onshore and offshore wind farms. Wind speed at sea is about 70% to 100% higher than onshore power, and it's much more constant, so I think the government should focus on that. I was reading a wind report form 2016, and, at that time, there were more than 27,000 onshore wind turbines and almost 1,000 offshore wind turbines in Germany. I wonder what that number is now? At the time, Germany was the number one in Europe for installing wind turbines, and number three in the whole world. Go Germany! It's something I'm really proud of. In this time when the whole world is worried about the climate, I'm proud to be from a country that's really doing something to help.

19th century illustration of Gutenberg and his printing press.

Germany + History = World War Two, right? That's all anyone thinks about when they think about the history of Germany. Guess what? Like every single place in the world, our history goes back further than the one event that everyone thinks defines us. Countries, leaders, empires... they all make mistakes, they all do things that generations to come look back on with shame. I know a lot about World War Two. Trust me! We study it in school all the time, and my grandparents talk about it a lot too. So, I don't want to talk about it now — I'd rather tell you something about Germany you don't know about.

Germans don't feel proud about World War Two, but there are plenty of things we do have reason to be proud of in our history. One you might have heard of is the Gutenberg Bible. Johannes Gutenberg was born in the year 1400 or thereabouts. No one knows exactly. He invented a printing press which brought the printed word to Europe. He was the first European to use movable type, which meant the letters and words and punctuation could all be moved around to print something else.

A facsimile of Gutenburg's Bible.

19

The Brothers Grimm

Something else from literary German antiquity are the stories of the Grimm brothers. Jacob and Wilhelm were born in the late 1700s, and they came from a big family, but it's just these two brothers that people know much about. These brothers studied medieval German literature, and, in time, they wrote their own stories. A lot of the stories they wrote were tales they'd been told as children or retellings of classic stories. Some people say the Grimm brothers just stole ideas from other writers, but you know, people say the same thing about Shakespeare, don't they?

The folk stories the Grimm brothers told were quite dark. They weren't like Disney stories that children enjoy today where there's a happy ending. These stories were horrifying! The children in the stories would have terrible things happen to them, such as being eaten. They were called 'warning tales' for children, so children would know what would happen to them if they were bad. I think you've probably heard of many of their stories, you just didn't know who wrote them. Here's some of them: *Cinderella, Rapunzel, Hansel and Gretel, Sleeping Beauty* and *The Goose Girl*.

Fun Fact

The Grimm brothers were philologists and librarians. They were working on compiling an ambitious German dictionary, but only got as far as the letter F before they died.

German History and Inventions

Ok, I'll stop talking about literature now. Can you tell I'm a bookworm? Well, I'm also quite interested in history, so I'm sure there are some other things I can tell you. Today, I read something in the newspaper about the Queen of the United Kingdom. Germany doesn't have a king or queen, but it did once. Did you know that? The German Monarchy ruled from 1871 to 1918, and during that time there were only three monarchs. The monarchy came about during the Franco-Prussian war, but they didn't call the leader a king, they called him an emperor.

Alois Alzheimer, German psychiatrist and neuropathologist.

If you want to search for information about the history of Germany, a lot of it is all about war. I don't think it's very interesting to tell you which wars Germany was involved in and what the dates were. Instead, I'm going to tell you about amazing German inventions. Ok, let's start with a medical one. In 1906, Alois Alzheimer discovered a disease that was named after him. I know about Alzheimer's disease because Lina's grandma has it, and I've visited her a few times. Every so often, Lina's grandma gets worse than she was before. She can't remember Lina's name anymore, and she can't do things like make a cup of tea by herself. Alzheimer's disease has been around for a long time, but they're still doing a lot of research into it to find out how to help people who are living with it.

Did you know?
It's estimated that more than 50 million people worldwide are living with Alzheimer's.

Kindergarten

It was a German man who created kindergarten. Isn't that a funny thought? Friedrich Fröbel understood that children have unique needs and capabilities. He basically invented the modern education system. His ideas weren't appreciated so much at the time, particularly in Germany, but the teachers who believed in him travelled all over the world and spread his ideas to new countries.

Early Washing Machine

Did you know that the washing machine was invented by a German person? Jacob Christian Schäffer invented a washing machine in 1767. Of course, it was a very early version and not at all like the washing machines that we use today! I know what you're thinking, you're thinking 'Hanna Luisa, you treat us to the most interesting and amazing facts!' Well, I think they're interesting, anyway. Who wants to learn about the same boring history that you study in schoolbooks when you can find out weird and wonderful things like who invented kindergarten and how we came to have printed books in Europe? Not me... give me the weird facts, any day!

fig. I

fig. II

Early washing machine illustrations.

Fun Fact
Jacob Christian Schäffer is also known for his works about Botany, entomology natural history, electricity, colours, and even optics!

Natural Wonders of Germany

Hallo, it's Hanna again. Have you had a good day? I've had a very good day. I don't normally like art classes at school. The thing I can see in my head never comes out right onto the paper, do you know what I mean? I can't think of unique, original things to paint or draw. But today we were doing botanical pictures. Botanical illustration is all about drawing plants and making them look accurate and lifelike. So, you don't need to imagine anything, you just copy what you can see.

We looked at the works of some famous botanical artists, especially German ones. Martin Schongauer was painting in the 1400s and his scientific illustrations are well known. I like the one of the peonies. Johann Jakob Walther was from the 1600s, and he drew many rare flowers and birds. Maria Sibylla Merian was a botanical artist who is still considered one of the best. In the late 1600s she painted exquisite flowers and insects. Her step-father was a botanical painter, and so were her daughters. I think that botanical illustration is so fascinating because it shows us clear pictures of the natural world in a time before photography.

Natural Wonders of Germany

Do you know what the national flower of Germany is? It's a cornflower. You might have heard of it because 'cornflower blue' is a shade of blue named after this flower. Blue isn't a very common colour in nature. How many animals or plants can you think of that are really blue? So, the cornflower is special because it has a vibrant and unique colour. Cornflower is also called bluebottle, hurtsickle, or Cyani flower. The cornflower is native to many different countries in Europe, but the flowers don't grow as much as they used to. I guess the cornflower is small and it's a wildflower, so people don't often bother to grow them in their gardens. Each flower has about fifty petals.

Cornflower in bloom during summer.

Chamomile tea is an herbal drink infused with dried chamomile flowers.

Matricaria chamomilla

Do you ever drink chamomile tea? Mama likes to drink it in the evening to relax. There are different types of chamomile, but there's one called Matricaria chamomilla which is the most famous one to use in tea and herbal remedies. This variety is also called German Chamomile because it grows a lot in Germany. The name isn't German though; it's Greek, and chamaimēlon means 'earth-apple.' They can grow to a similar height to the cornflower and are also a wild flower. Have you seen chamomile growing before? The petals are white, the middle is a buttery yellow, and they smell amazing.

German Trees

Botanical artists can draw trees as well as flowers. Do you know what trees we have in Germany? Did you know that the Christmas tree tradition started in Germany? We call it a Tannenbaum. The tradition started in the 1500s and, in the 19th century, other European countries were having special trees at Christmastime, too. We have many evergreen trees in Europe and at Christmas will usually use an evergreen conifer, such as a spruce, pine, or fir tree.

Where I live, in North Rhine-Westphalia, the trees look so bare in the winter. Of course, we have some evergreens, but many of the trees will lose their leaves when the weather is cold and frosty. Snow dusts the tree branches, and the squirrels you usually see playing on the tree branches are all hidden away in hibernation.

One popular tree you can find all around this part of Europe is the common juniper, which is a conifer. They have a far-reaching spread but the trees aren't very tall. They only reach a height of about 20 feet. A much bigger tree is the European silver fir, which can grow to more than 160 feet. These trees can live for about 300 years. If you want to see the silver fir, you should go to the Black Forest.

Fun Fact
The mountainous forest covers an area of 6,009.2 km2 (2,320.2 sq mi).

Schwarzwald, also known as The Black Forest is a mountain range in Baden-Württemberg, southwest Germany.

I was reading about something very unusual in Germany to do with trees. I'm sure you know the swastika symbol was used by the Nazi party in World War II and is associated with antisemitism, though of course the symbol itself is much older than that and has different meanings around the world. Well, around the late 1930s, a forest of trees was planted with this symbol hidden in the forest. Once the trees were big and grown and the leaves changed colour in the autumn, some of the trees were a different colour than the others. Their leaves made a picture in the trees, and it looked just like a swastika.

The forest swastika wasn't known about for a long time because you can only see it from above the trees, like out of a plane, and only during certain times of the year. In 1995, people were worried that it was a bad image, and so they tried to destroy some of the trees to ruin the picture. However, it was unsuccessful because so many trees needed to be cut down, and some of them grew back. But then they tried again in December in the year 2000 and managed to cut down enough of the trees to break the bad image.

German Wildlife

If you go to the Black Forest, look out for the Black Forest horse. This breed is now endangered although it was once indispensable to the German people. The horse worked on farms and in fields. I think they're wonderful creatures. The horses are a chestnut colour, though often a much darker brown, and they have a long mane of silvery-white hair. I hope this breed of horse doesn't go extinct. The wild horse of Germany is extinct in the wild, but there are some in captivity. Another animal in danger in Germany is the European mink, which is critically endangered.

Other wild animals in Germany are the gray wolf and the red fox. I've never seen these animals in the wild but I've visited zoos where they lived.

The Country of Poets and Thinkers

Do you know anyone who likes poetry? Some people think that poetry isn't cool. There are kids at school who say poetry is lame. But I think poetry is nice, don't you? Papa likes poetry a lot. He has a book of poems next to his bed and reads one every night before he goes to sleep. I think he's a true German! In the past, Germany was known as the country of poets and thinkers. That's a good description of Papa!

What do you think about German culture and German people? There are both positive and negative things that we are known for. Some people say that Germans are humourless. It's not true that we don't enjoy to laugh and joke, but I think it's true that we only do it in certain places. Mama says that in her workplace she doesn't share jokes with her colleagues. At work, Germans are professional and hardworking. The same is true in school. We can laugh and play at break time, but in lessons we should be serious.

I think the serious nature of the German people has led to us being well respected. We have been rated as one of the most valued nations in the world, and Germany is also said to have had, at one point, the most positive influence in the whole world. Germany is at the forefront of many sectors, and we try to have a very equal society. We have taken big steps toward creating equality in our society. We are at the front for supporting disability rights, gender equality, and for the LGBTQ+ society.

German Games

Did you know that Germany publishes more board games than any other country per capita? You might find it funny that a population who doesn't like to joke much actually really enjoys playing fun games. In Germany, there are many people who invent Eurogames. These are German-style board games. Did you play board games when you were small? Maybe you thought they were not board-games but boring-games, right? Well, Eurogames are different. People love them all over the world, especially adults.

One popular Eurogame is Carcassonne. It's named after the medieval town in southern France. A well-known game inventor, Klaus-Jürgen Wrede, designed the game. This game is a great modern board game because it has no board at the start — the game is to build the board, piece by piece. You get points for building certain things, like roads or cities, and putting your wooden meeples (people) onto it.

CARCASSONNE

Fun Fact

For the first five years, Germans won the Carcassonne World Championships. From 2011 onwards, they've been won by people from The Netherlands, Japan, the Czech Republic, Poland, and Greece.

Another great German game is The Settlers of Catan. It's usually just called 'Settlers' or 'Catan'. This game is special because it was the first Eurogame that became popular outside of Germany. It was developed in 1995, and by 2015 it had been translated into more than 30 languages and sold over 22 million copies. It's a strategy game like Carcassonne. The board is built by chance at the start of the game, and you build roads, settlements, and cities, and you get other cards for victory points.

German Poets and Philosophers

I told you that Germany is called the country of poets and thinkers, so I guess I should tell you about some famous people from these categories, right? Born in 1749, Johann Wolfgang von Goethe was a writer of all sorts. He's a distinguished author of German literature, so his work is often studied by German schoolchildren. Of course, I know about Goethe from my father, who loves his work. His first collection of poetry was *Annette*, and it was poetry about love. However, his most famous work is a play called *Faust* and is about a man who strikes a deal with the devil.

A more modern German poet was Rainer Maria Rilke, who lived from 1875 to 1926. He was actually Bohemian-Austrian and born in Switzerland, but he wrote in the German language and is considered one of our greatest poets. He was a modern poet but wrote about archaic things. He often wrote about Greek mythology and mystical things. He also wrote poems that we would call 'meta' today, with the topic of being a poet and the work of a poet. His poetry was very lyrical, meaning it was like a song.

Johann Wolfgang von Goethe monument in Saxony, Germany.

Did you know?

On December 29, 1926, Rilke died of leukemia and chose this poem for his epitaph:

"Rose, o pure contradiction, desire
to be no one's sleep beneath so many lids."

Immanuel Kant

From poetry to philosophy. I can't skip the opportunity to tell you about Immanuel Kant... haha, get it? Can't... Kant... ok, I told you already that Germans don't make good comedians! Anyway... Kant was living in the Age of Enlightenment. These days, schoolchildren studying philosophy will learn about Kantianism, which is basically all the stuff that Kant talked about.

I don't know much about Kant's theories because we haven't studied him in school yet, but I know a few funny facts. Papa said that Kant was big fan of the writer Goethe. Every day after dinner, Kant used to take a walk. He was so regular in his habits that the local people could tell them time by when they saw him! Kant is said to have sat in a big oven to concentrate and block out distractions, particularly the works of other philosophers that he disagreed with. Sounds pretty bonkers, right? I love crazy people from history, don't you?

Colourful wooden toys on display in Munich, Germany.

Celebrations in Germany

It's getting close to Christmastime. Are you excited? I am. Christmas is a very important festival in Germany. I already told you that Christmas trees basically come from Germany, so you can understand the winter holiday is important to us. This year, Mama says we are going to have an eco-friendly Christmas. At first, I was worried that we would be having a vegetarian Christmas meal, but Mama said I shouldn't worry — we will eat the same things for Christmas dinner, but this year we will buy them in ecologically friendly shops.

I know that, around the world, Christmas is a very commercial thing now. A big focus is on presents instead of the important things like spending time with family, doing nice things for other people, etc. Because I'm an only child, Mama and Papa can afford to buy expensive Christmas presents for me. They buy nice presents for their friends and our neighbours, too. But this year, we're going to do things differently.

Mama and I have been making an advent calendar. In German we call this an Adventskalendar. I usually have an advent calendar from the shop. The same for you? Mama says the shop bought ones aren't good because the chocolate comes on a plastic tray, and it's part of the throwaway culture. So, we're making one that we can use every year. Mama bought a big piece of green felt which we cut into the shape of a Christmas trees. Then we cut baubles and stocking shapes out of more felt, and we're sewing them onto the tree to make little pockets. Each pocket will have a chocolate in it, and next year we can fill it with more chocolate.

Homemade adventskalendar.

Christmas Gifts

We won't be buying expensive gifts this year. Mama says a gift from the home is a gift from the heart, so we're going to give handmade presents to our friends and neighbours. Mama and I have been baking lebkuchen. Perhaps you've tried this German delicacy? You've probably tried it but don't know what it's called. In English, people sometimes call it a Christmas Biscuit or Christmas Gingerbread. I think lebkuchen is better than gingerbread. It's made with honey, and the texture is much softer. It doesn't hurt your teeth. The traditional lebkuchen is shaped like a heart and has plain white icing for decoration. They're köstlich! That means delicious!

We will also make some stollen. Unlike Christmas cake, which you can make months in advance, German stollen is a sweet bread best enjoyed fresh. Many people bake stollen in the shape of a Christmas wreath, but you can also just bake it like a plain loaf. This bread doesn't need jam on it because it already has so many different flavours and ingredients. Orange peel, almonds, marzipan, cinnamon, rum, raisins, and cardamom are common flavours for the stollen mixture. It originates in Germany and is particularly popular in Dresden.

Stollen, a traditional German bread made of nuts, fruits and spices. It is usually eaten in Christmas.

Christmas Markets

I feel like Germany invented nearly all the cool things we do at Christmas. Did you know that Christmas Markets originated in Germany too? We have so many names for the markets at Christmas time. Weihnachtsmarkt is probably the closest translation to Christmas Market. Another name is Christkindlmarkt which means 'Christ Child Market.' But Christ Child doesn't mean the baby Jesus — it means the spirit of Christmas, sort of like an angel. I know, it's complicated, right?

Christmas Market in Berlin, Germany

Did you know that the first Christmas Markets in Germany happened in the Late Middle Ages? As the name suggests, that was AGES ago! These days, the markets sell everything, from biscuits to soap, from candles to toys. It's a great place to go shopping for Christmas presents, but this year we aren't doing so much shopping, so we will just enjoy the atmosphere and get something nice to eat. Traditional stalls at the market sell things like lebkuchen, stollen, Bratwurst sausage, Nussknacker (which is a decorated nutcracker, used to open nuts which are popular to eat at Christmas), and my mother's favourite seasonal drink — which is mulled wine.

Kinderpunsch, an alcohol-free drink made with a blend of fruit tea and a variety of spices.

Fun Fact
A non-alcoholic version of Glühwein, called Kinderpunsch, is also available for children.

Oktoberfest Fairgrounds, Munich, Germany

Unusual Festivals

German people love to have a good time, even if the rest of the world think we don't have any humour. Have you heard of any special German festivals? I'm sure you've heard of Oktoberfest. It takes place each year in Munich. The festival is basically all about drinking beer. About 7 million people attends the festival. Together, they drink about 8 million litres of beer. That's a lot of beer! The festival is huge. People sit in massive tents, and I imagine it's very noisy.

Many people going to Oktoberfest dress up in the traditional German costume, called Lederhose and Dirndl. Women wear the dirndl, which are knee-length dresses with a tight bodice, and under that you wear a white shirt. You should also wear a long apron at your waist, and depending which side you knot the apron on, it tells people if you are single or married. I think it's a very funny tradition!

Fun Fact

Men wear the lederhosen. These are knee-length trousers made from leather which would have been good for farm workers. The trousers have suspenders which go over the shoulder, and they wear a checked shirt under that. Sometimes they wear a white hat with the outfit but not always. What do you think about the national dress of Germany?

Schwarzwälder Kirschtorte or Black Forest cake, chocolate sponge cake with rich cherry filling.

Schwarzwälder Kirschtorte for the Sweet Tooth

Do you have a sweet tooth? I know I do. I love sweet snacks, puddings, and desserts. I seriously have no control over myself around sweet things! When I was little, I ate too much candy, and the dentist was worried about my teeth. These days Mama keeps a strict watch on how much sweet stuff I have. Now, we usually just have something sweet on the weekends. But that means it's a real treat, and I can have something delicious.

One German treat I love is, also called Black Forest Cake. People think it's named after the Black Forest in Germany, but it's named after the liquor that comes from that area. There's a rule that you can't call it Schwarzwälder Kirschtorte unless it contains kirschwasser, which is the name of a spirit made from sour cherries. Have you tried a black forest gateau? It's chocolate sponge, layered with whipped cream and amazing cherries. I think it's underrated. People think it's an old-fashioned cake and it isn't so popular, but I think it's incredible.

SCHWARZWÄLDER

KIRSCHSWASSER

Popular German Puddings

A pudding that is more popular, particularly in northern Germany, is Rote Grütze. The name means 'red pudding,' and it's also popular in Denmark. You can make it just with red currants, but I think the best ones have several different types of red fruit: cherries, raspberries, strawberries, black currants, or blackberries. I think you basically just heat up the fruit and add some sugar, and then it's served with ice-cream, cream, custard, or vanilla sauce. I tell Mama that this one is a healthy pudding because it's just fruit, which is good for you, but of course fruit contains a lot of natural sugars!

A strange pudding you might not have heard of is Spaghettieis. It looks like spaghetti, right? Well, this is a pudding that's made to look just like a bowl of spaghetti! You'd get such a surprise if you took a bite and thought it would be hot! The pasta is made from vanilla ice-cream which you put through a potato ricer, and it comes out in long strands like spaghetti. The tomato sauce over the top is actually strawberry sauce. To top it off, you sprinkle white chocolate or coconut flakes over it to look like parmesan cheese. It's a crazy dessert, and I love to have it when we go to a restaurant.

Rote Grütze or red pudding.

Roasted wurst or sausages.

Savoury, Yet Delicious

German food isn't all about sweet stuff, though. That's just what I like! Germany is famous for several dishes that have nothing to do with pudding. I guess you've heard about German sausages? In Germany, we like to eat meat, especially pork. Can you guess how many types of sausage there are in Germany? Many, many different types. You could never know all their names, I promise you. We call sausages 'wurst,' and the most famous one is bratwurst. Wurst is also the name we give to cold cuts of meat, which are also popular.

In Germany, we often eat meat at breakfast, particularly on the weekend. A small German breakfast would just be some bread or toast, and of course in recent years children prefer to eat cereal. If you're having a big breakfast in Germany, it will be something like this: bread will be served with jam, honey, butter, or cheese, and you can choose cold cuts like ham, salami, or meat spreads, and to drink you can have tea, coffee, hot or cold chocolate or maybe some fruit juice. We usually just have toast with some butter and jam on the weekdays, but on the weekends, we have a big breakfast. If Papa is in a hurry and needs to go to work early, he might buy a belegte Brötchen from the bakery — this is a sort of breakfast sandwich.

Healthy, homemade cereal is a favorite breakfast for many German children.

A dish my father likes is Bratkartoffeln. It's quite simple — just boiled potato which you slice thinly and then fry with oil, bacon, and onion. It's not very healthy, but it's hearty and is an easy side dish to have with something else. A German dish that isn't quick and easy is Sauerbraten. This is something we have on a special occasion. It's a slow cooked piece of good quality meat, and you can serve it with traditional egg noodles, which we call Spätzle.

Bratkartoffeln, or German Fries made with potatoes slices and other ingredients such as herbs, onion, or bacon bits.

You probably know about Schnitzel, right? In an old film called *The Sound of Music* there's a song called 'My Favourite Things,' and the lady says that one of her favourite things is schnitzel with noodles. She probably means schnitzel with Spätzle! Anyway, schnitzel is a thin piece of meat that is deep fried in breadcrumbs. It's delicious, but not very healthy, of course! Traditionally it's called Wiener Schnitzel and made using veal, but these days many people eat it with pork, or even chicken or something vegetarian like cheese.

Homemade German Schnitzel.

Sauerkraut, a German side dish made of fermented raw cabbage.

Healthy German Food

You must think that German people just like to eat sweets and meat! Ok, let me tell you about something healthy. In Germany, we love asparagus. It's not always been a popular vegetable around the world, but in Germany we love it. Our favourite way to serve it is in a buttery white sauce... which of course makes it less healthy! Sauerkraut is a vegetable dish you might have heard of. It basically means 'sour cabbage,' and it has a strong, distinctive taste. Onions and root vegetables are also popular. We eat a lot of carrots and tomatoes, too. For fruit, in Germany we love to eat apples, bananas, and grapes. So, we do eat some healthy things, too!

A postage stamp featuring the German archaeolgist Heinrich Schliemann.

The Germans you Should Know About

Do your parents have idols? You know, like musicians they listen to all the time or actors they loved when they were little? My parents definitely have idols, but they're not your usual celebrities! I already told you that Papa is an archaeologist and works in the Mettmann Neanderthal Museum, didn't I? Well, you mightn't be too surprised to learn that many of his idols are in his field of work.

German Archaeologists and Scientists

Papa's favourite archaeologist is Heinrich Schliemann, who lived in the 1800s. He's a pretty impressive one because he basically discovered prehistoric Greece. He came from a poor family but worked hard and, unusually for the time, he travelled all over the world. In the 1800s, it wasn't usual for a poor boy who worked in the grocery shop to become an educated man who could travel to China, Japan, Syria, and Scandinavia!

Fun Fact

After studying archaeology in Paris, Schliemann had many theories about ancient worlds that were undiscovered. In 1871, he discovered Troy, which was the setting of the Trojan War and that story about the trojan horse. He also excavated Mycenae, which was another ancient city in Greece.

Another of Papa's heroes is Albert Einstein. Did you know that Einstein was born in Germany? However, he renounced his German citizenship when he was a young man and become a Swiss national instead. He was one of the smartest people who ever lived. Einstein taught himself all sorts of things when he was still a boy. He was particularly good at math and physics, and he taught himself things like algebra, geometry, and calculus.

Einstein developed the theory of relativity. This idea eventually earned him the Nobel Prize for Physics. I don't really understand a lot of that science stuff, but Papa says it's fascinating!

Albert Einstein

German Composers and Musicians

I think most of Mama's idols are from the world of music. She can't play any musical instruments, but she loves to listen to music. People my age often think that classical music is boring, but I think they're wrong. Classical music is so versatile. It can be fast or slow, relaxing or exciting, tuneful or crazy. Some of the most famous and best-known classical musicians come from Germany.

Let's start with Bach. I bet you know this one, but do you know how to pronounce it? If you just read it, perhaps you think it sounds like 'batch.' But it sounds more like 'back' or 'bark' if you say it properly. He worked during the Baroque period, which was from about 1600 to 1750. Bach was one of the greatest composers the Western world has ever seen, and while he could play many instruments, he was best known as an organist.

Statute of Johann Sebastian Bach in Leipzig, Germany.

Bach was dedicated to his craft. I know this because, when he was 20 years old, he walked 280 miles just so he could attend a classical concert. Only a truly devoted musician would go to that much effort! He was talented, but I don't think he was a very friendly person. Bach was always arguing with people and once had a fight with one of his music students. He was once put in prison for a whole month because he quit his job and joined a rival performance group, which seems like a bad punishment to me! There are plenty of stories of Bach not getting on well with people in the music world. Overall, I think that although Bach was successful, he had a difficult life, and he met an unpleasant end, too.

The Beethoven Monument on the Munsterplatz in Bonn, Germany.

Ludwig van Beethoven

Another German musician you might have heard of is Ludwig van Beethoven. Beethoven was born in 1770 and died in 1827, so like Bach, he had quite a short life. He had been ill for a while and nobody really knows exactly what he died from, although he certainly had liver damage from excessive alcohol consumption. Around 20,000 people attended his funeral procession, so it's clear that Beethoven was a celebrity of the day! Like Bach, Beethoven didn't always get on well with his contemporaries. What was it with these musical guys and not being friendly to others?

Beethoven was a composer and pianist. During his lifetime, Beethoven composed nine symphonies. His most famous piece is called *Für Elise* and is a popular piece for pianists to learn. The name means 'For Elise' but it's not known who he wrote it for — scholars have come up with three women whose name or nickname was Elise, and it could have been any of them that Beethoven was composing the song for. The piano piece was written in A minor and was composed in 1810.

German Authors

I'm a bookworm and love reading so most of my German idols are authors. The one you've probably heard of is Anne Frank, who was a Dutch-Jewish diarist and was born in Germany. A more modern author I like is Cornelia Funke. She's most famous for her *Inkheart* trilogy which we call Tintenwelt-Trilogie in German. Her books were published in the 2000s, are still popular for fantasy lovers, and have sold over 20 million copies worldwide!

Charles Bukowski is a German-American novelist who Papa likes. Bukowski wrote books, but he also wrote short stories and poetry, which of course my father is interested in too. Bukowski moved to America when he was only three years old but, despite this, his work was very popular in Germany, particularly after his death in 1994. Another author who was born in Germany but moved away when he was three is Gyles Brandreth. Most of his books have been about puzzles, jokes, and words, and he often appears on British TV shows such as *QI* and *Countdown*. Gyles in a very clever man but is also a comedian — a good combination, in my opinion!

A view of Neuschwanstein Castle in Hohenschwangau, Germany.

Are you trying to decide where to visit in Germany? There are plenty of places that tourists always go to, so they're busy, but there are many off the beaten track destinations that you've probably never heard of. My best friend Lina has a big family, so it can be stressful going to busy places. She likes to visit small towns and villages. But I'm an only child, so my parents find it easy taking me to popular locations. I think it's best if I tell you about both types of place!

The Romantic Road

There's a place in Germany that was basically invented to be a tourist attraction. It's called the Romantic Road and describes a 350 kilometre (220 mi) route in southern Germany. I guess you're wondering what's so special about a road, right? Well the Romantische Straße was made into a tourist destination in the 1950s by travel agents who wanted to boost tourism in the area. Traveling north from Füssen to Würzburg, you travel through about thirty top tourism spots in the area. Some of these are stunning castles which look like they're straight out of a Disney movie. Neuschwanstein Castle is one of the best-known ones you will see. It's truly beautiful, and it looks like it's floating above the treetops because it's so tall.

> ### Fun Fact
> Neuschwanstein Castle is fairly modern. It was completed in 1886 and opened to the public almost immediately. It was built as a home for the king, but he only slept there for 11 nights before his death, after which the castle plans were simplified.

When travelling the Romantic Road, people often stop in a town called Rothenburg ob der Tauber. It's one of the best places in Germany to see a preserved medieval town, like stepping back in time. The streets are cobbled, the houses are made of timber, and it looks like a charming village from a fairy tale. It's the kind of place where you want time to just walk around and soak up the atmosphere. Oh, and if you like unusual museums, the town has a Criminal Museum which has some artefacts that were used to torture prisoners!

Rothenburg ob der Tauber a town in Bavaria, Germany, well known for its well-preserved medieval old town.

Museum island on Spree River in center Berlin, Germany.

The Capital City

Most people who come to Germany will visit Berlin, the capital. You could honestly spend years trying to see and do all these is to experience in Berlin. The capital has about 140 museums and more than 400 art galleries, so there is no shortage of cultural experiences. If museums are something you want to see, head to Museum Island. On the Spree River, there's an island where the northern half of the island is covered with museums. It's been a UNESCO World Heritage Site since 1999. The island was dedicated to art and science by King Frederick William IV of Prussia in 1841, but there had been exhibitions there before that time. There are five museums you can enter with one ticket, so it's a good option if you want to see a lot in one place!

In Berlin, there are many other things to see and do. If you're interested in history, the Holocaust Memorial Museum is a place you should visit. The Brandenburg Gate is another must-visited destination. I like Berlin Zoo because it's very green, and you forget that you're in the middle of a huge city! If you want to see outdoor spaces in Berlin, parks and gardens that I recommend include the Britzer Garden, Treptower Park, and Mauer Park.

Brandenburg Gate, Berlin, Germany.

Off the Beaten Track

Last year, Lina went on holiday to Friedrichshafen, a city down in the far south of Germany which sits on the northern shore of Lake Constance. The city is famous for all the airplane builders and designers who came from there, and there's even an aviation museum called the Zeppelin Museum. It's the world's largest aviation collection, and they went there because Lina's brother loves everything to do with old airplanes.

Night view of Friedrichshafen at Lake Constance.

Did you know?

The museum houses a full-sized replica of the Hindenburg, a German passenger airship which caught on fire in 1937, killing 36 people. The tragedy was captured on film with a live commentary by Herbert Morrison, an American radio journalist.

A place I recently found out about is called Odenwald, and I'd really like to go there. It's a low mountain range which spans the states of Hesse, Bavaria, and Baden-Württemberg. I've never been hiking or camping before — not on a proper adventure, anyway — and Odenwald is the perfect place to go if you like those things. It's known for its clean air and stunning views. There are also many legends from the Odenwald area, such as the ghosts of knights and medieval ladies that appear in local castles, and even apparitions of the devil! There are two mountains which are over 600m tall, but most of them are small and offer great views of lakes and other bodies of water. I've seen photographs of amazing rock formations in the gorges that I would love to see. Perhaps I can persuade Papa and Mama to take me there in the summer!

Rathaus Michelstadt im Odenwald.

Lighthouse with Thatched Roof in the island of Sylt.

Another undiscovered area I've read about is called Sylt. It's the most northern island in Germany and though my country isn't famous for its beaches or coastal destinations, this is one I'd love to go to. The sandy beach is 40-kilo-metres long (25 miles), and it looks like a great place to relax, although it doesn't get super-hot there in the summer so I'm not sure I'd want to sunbathe! Sylt is part of the Frisian Islands and you can see the traditional thatched cottages around the island.

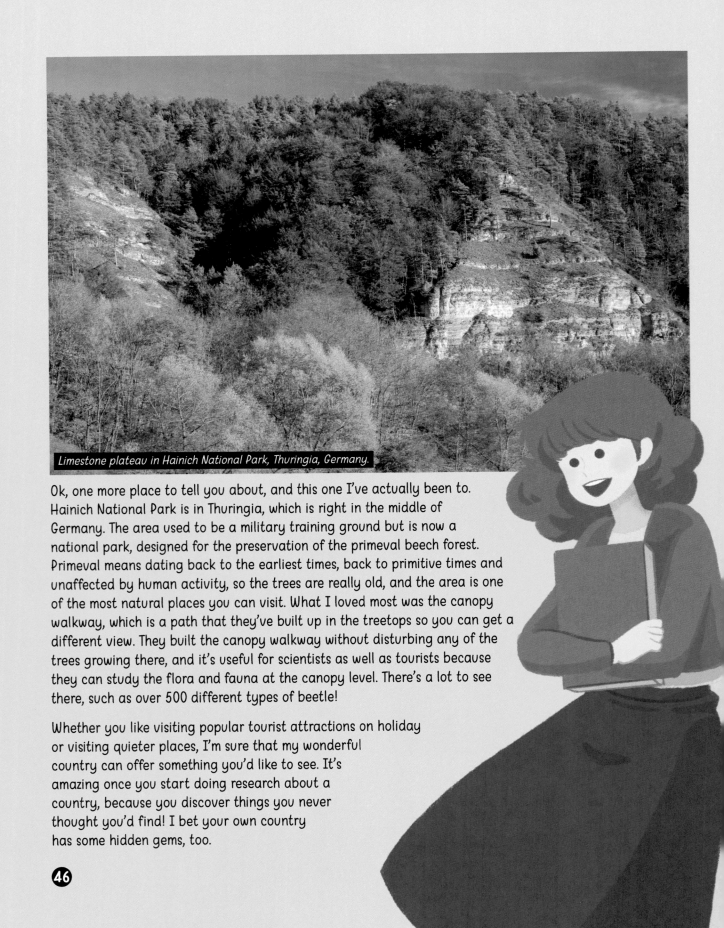

Limestone plateau in Hainich National Park, Thuringia, Germany.

Ok, one more place to tell you about, and this one I've actually been to. Hainich National Park is in Thuringia, which is right in the middle of Germany. The area used to be a military training ground but is now a national park, designed for the preservation of the primeval beech forest. Primeval means dating back to the earliest times, back to primitive times and unaffected by human activity, so the trees are really old, and the area is one of the most natural places you can visit. What I loved most was the canopy walkway, which is a path that they've built up in the treetops so you can get a different view. They built the canopy walkway without disturbing any of the trees growing there, and it's useful for scientists as well as tourists because they can study the flora and fauna at the canopy level. There's a lot to see there, such as over 500 different types of beetle!

Whether you like visiting popular tourist attractions on holiday or visiting quieter places, I'm sure that my wonderful country can offer something you'd like to see. It's amazing once you start doing research about a country, because you discover things you never thought you'd find! I bet your own country has some hidden gems, too.

CONCLUSION

When I started telling you about my country, I wondered if I'd find enough to say. I mean, I've only travelled to a very small percentage of this big, beautiful country, so I didn't know if I'd have enough experiences to share with you. But the process of researching my homeland has been amazing. When people think about Germany, the same things spring to mind — our tricolour flag, Hitler and the war, Oktoberfest, German sausages… but of course, there is so much more to a country than what you can name from the top of your head.

What have you learned about Germany that has been particularly interesting? Did you know that Germany was so diverse and amazing? Personally, I've discovered things about my country that I didn't know before. I've learned about places I'd love to visit, and reminded myself of delicious German dishes that I don't eat very often. This journey hasn't just been for you as I, Hanna Luisa, have also learned a lot! Well, whatever you've found interesting, I hope you're enthusiastic about your trip to Germany and would like to do many of the things I've mentioned. Have a great trip!

Which parts of Germany did you like the most and why?

_____

_____

_____

_____

_____

_____

_____

_____

_____

_____

What activities did you enjoy most and why?

_____

_____

_____

_____

_____

_____

_____

_____

_____

Now, to our pop quiz! Good luck!

What is the shore length of Lake Constance?
(a) 175 km (108 mi)
(b) 210 km (130 mi)
(c) 273 km (170 mi)

(answer (c) — 273 km (170 mi))

Which of these German or German-writing poets won the Nobel Prize for Literature in 1946?
(a) Johann Wolfgang von Goethe
(b) Hermann Hesse
(c) Rainer Maria Rilke

(answer (b) — Hermann Hesse)

Which state in Germany has the least amount of wind turbines?
(a) Hesse
(b) Bavaria
(c) Berlin

(answer (c) — Berlin)

How many types of German sausage are there?
(a) About 100
(b) About 500
(c) About 1,500

(answer (c) — About 1,500)

How many Aldi stores are there in Germany?
(a) Fewer than 2,000
(b) About 3,000
(c) More than 4,000

(answer (c) — More than 4,000)

Which of these is a place in Germany where you can enjoy great skiing in the winter?
(a) The Black Forest
(b) The Blue Forest
(c) The Green Forest

(answer (a) — The Black Forest)

How long was the biggest stollen loaf ever baked?
(a) 42.9 metres (140.73 ft) long
(b) 58.4 metres (191.6 ft) long
(c) 72.1 metres (237 ft) long

(answer (c) — 72.1 metres (237 ft) long)

Apfelkuchen is a popular German dessert, but what does it mean in English?
(a) Apple Pie
(b) Chocolate Cake
(c) Coffee Ice-cream

(answer (a) — Apple Pie)

How many people visit the Neuschwanstein Castle in Hohenschwangau each year?
(a) 1.1 million
(b) 1.3 million
(c) 1.5 million

(answer (b) — 1.3 million)

What is the most famous historical artefact found on Museum Island?
(a) A complete Tyrannosaurus rex skeleton
(b) The Rosetta Stone
(c) A bust of the Egyptian queen Nefertiti

(answer (c) — A bust of the Egyptian queen Nefertiti)

I have thoroughly enjoyed this journey through France with you.
Feel free to visit us at www.dinobibi.com and check out our other titles!

Dinobibi Travel for Kids

Dinobibi History for Kids

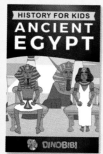 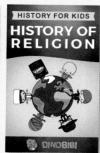   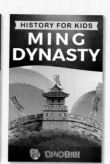

   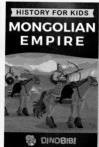 

Made in the USA
Las Vegas, NV
18 March 2024

87359800R00031